Firebase Storage for Angular

A reliable file upload solution for your applications

Abdelfattah Ragab

Firebase Storage for Angular

A reliable file upload solution for your applications

Abdelfattah Ragab

Introduction

Welcome to the book "Firebase Storage for Angular: A reliable file upload solution for your applications".
In this book, I explain how you can integrate Firebase Storage into your Angular application.
One of the pain points in many applications is where to store the application files. Whether you want to upload the product images for your e-commerce store or allow users of your social media application to upload files, etc. You need a reliable file storage provider to manage your files.
Fortunately, Firebase Storage comes to the rescue.
By the end of this book, you will be able to manage files freely from your application and handle all kinds of scenarios.
Let us get started.

What is Cloud Storage for Firebase?

Cloud Storage for Firebase is a powerful and cost-effective object storage service designed for managing user-generated content such as images, audio, video and other files. It is based on the Google Cloud infrastructure and offers scalability and reliability for developers working on mobile, web and server applications.

Google account

You should have a google account.
1. Sign in to your account.
2. Open firebase website.
3. Go to the console.

Create a project

1. Start a new firebase project.
2. Give it a name and continue.

Enable Cloud Storage

In the firebase console, navigate to the storage section and click on Get Started.

You need to set up your Cloud Billing Account, if not already done.

Create a Storage Bucket

During setup, you will be prompted to create a cloud storage bucket. Choose a unique name for your bucket, select the appropriate storage class and specify the storage location that best suits your needs.

Configure Security Rules

Check and configure the security rules for the cloud storage. Firebase requires authentication for read and write operations by default. You can customize these rules depending on the requirements of your application, e.g. allow public access during development.

The Backend

As with all of our major applications, I will set up a backend server in the middle between the Angular application and the Firebase server to protect the business logic from changes and hide our API keys.

I will create three modules: db, rooms and storage. The upload logic is implemented in the storage module, but I have created two more modules to give you a broad idea of how to use it in real life.

I assume a hotel booking application, and you as the owner want to upload images for the hotel room.
I have also created the db module to serve as a replacement for the database. For the sake of simplicity, let us just push the newly added room into the room array.

Preview

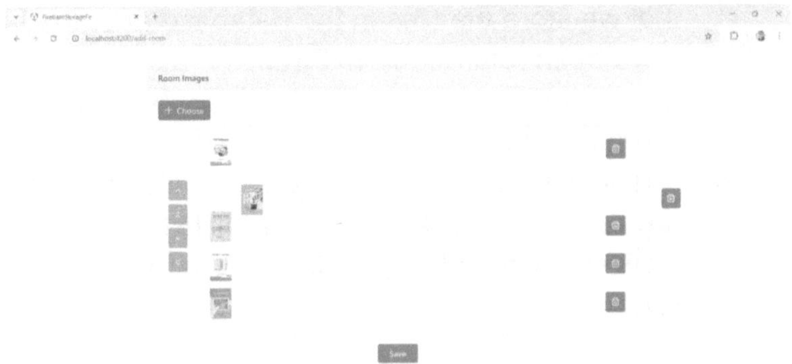

We will build a multi file upload solution and I will use the primeng orderlist component to allow ordering the files.

How does it work!

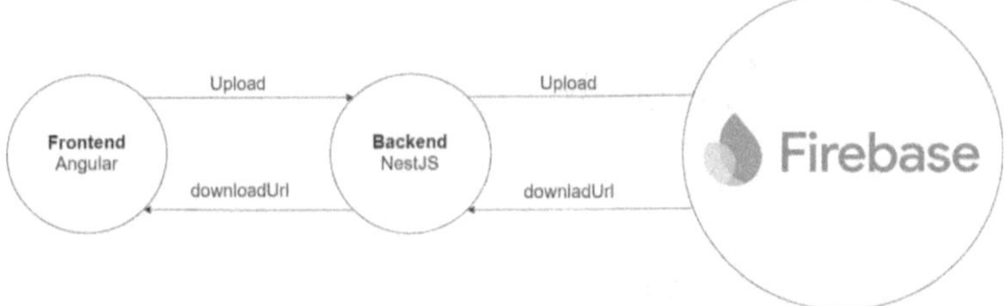

1. You select files on your computer that will be sent to the NestJS backend server.
2. The NestJS backend server sends the files to the Firebase server.
3. The Firebase server uploads the files and responds with the DownloadUrl.
4. NestJS stores the details of the uploaded files in the database (in our case in the db array). Note

that we store the files in the database after they have been returned from Firebase, as they now have the DownloadUrl required to preview and download the files.

5. The final step is to return the saved file array to the Angular application, which will read the DownloadUrl and display the files in the order list.

Source code

You can find the code example at `https://books.abdelfattah-ragab.com` Download, unzip and run. Don't forget to `npm install`.

Debug Enabled

In the Nest application, you can start troubleshooting by clicking on the "Run" menu" → "Start Debugging".
This works because I added a **launch.json** file in the **.vscode** folder. It contains the configuration for NestJS debugging. Simply add this file to any of your NestJS applications to enable debugging.

Install Dependencies

We need to install Firebase, uuid and dotenv:.
`npm i firebase uuid dotenv`

I will use `uuid` to generate unique names for uploaded files and `dotenv` to read the keys from the **.env** file.

Install `@types/multer` **as a dev dependency.**
```
npm i @types/multer --save-dev
```

`.eslintrc.js`

Customize the configuration of the **.eslintrc.js** file, otherwise you will get a lot of warnings. Since I don't need it for this application, I will delete its content and replace it with an empty object as follows:
```
module.exports = {};
```

Firebase Keys

Add the firebase keys to the **.env** file
```
FIREBASE_APIKEY=AIz..
FIREBASE_AUTHDOMAIN=fb-sto..
FIREBASE_PROJECTID=fb-sto..
FIREBASE_STORAGEBUCKET=fb-sto..
FIREBASE_MESSAGINGSENDERID=415..
FIREBASE_APPID=1:4150..
```

DB Module

For simplicity I will create a db module with arrays to save files and room details instead of connecting to the database.
Create a new module for db as follows:

```
nest generate module modules/db
```

DB Service

Create a new service for db as follows:

```
nest generate service modules/db
```

It will have the following arrays:

```
private rooms: Room[] = [];
private files: File[] = [];
private roomFiles: RoomFile[] = [];
```

Similar to the database, we have an array for rooms and another for files, with the roomFiles array taking on the role of the relational tables in the database. It simply defines which files belong to which rooms.

The dbService will have methods to add and delete entries.

Storage Module

Create a new module for storage as follows:

```
nest generate module modules/storage
```

Storage Service

Create a new service for storage as follows:
```
nest generate service modules/storage
```

Storage Controller

Create a new controller for storage as follows:
```
nest generate controller modules/storage
```

File Entity

```
export class File {
  id: number;
  originalName: string;
  mimeType: string;
  downloadUrl: string;
  fullPath: string;
  size: number;
}
```

File Service

Create a new service for file as follows:
```
nest generate service
modules/storage/file --flat --no-spec
```

It will have methods to add, get and delete files. It uses the dbService as a repository.

```typescript
import { Injectable, NotFoundException }
from '@nestjs/common';
import { File } from './file.entity';
import { DbService } from
'../db/db.service';

@Injectable()
export class FileService {
  constructor(private readonly
dbService: DbService) {}

  async saveFile(file: File) {
    return this.dbService.addFile(file);
  }

  async getFile(fileId: number) {
    return
this.dbService.getFile(fileId);
  }

  async deleteFile(fileId: number) {
    const found =
this.dbService.getFile(fileId);
    if (found) {
      this.dbService.deleteFile(fileId);
      return found;
    } else {
```

```
      throw new NotFoundException('File
Not Found!');
    }
  }
}
```

When I upload a new file to Firebase storage, I store its details in the file service so that I can easily access it later and connect it to the various resources in our applications, such as rooms. The physical file is hosted by Firebase, but we have full information about it stored in our database.

Implement `StorageService`

First declare the api keys properties as follows:
```
apiKey =
`${process.env.FIREBASE_APIKEY}`;
authDomain =
`${process.env.FIREBASE_AUTHDOMAIN}`;
projectId =
`${process.env.FIREBASE_PROJECTID}`;
storageBucket =
`${process.env.FIREBASE_STORAGEBUCKET}`;
messagingSenderId =
`${process.env.FIREBASE_MESSAGINGSENDERI
D}`;
appId = `${process.env.FIREBASE_APPID}`;

firebaseConfig = {
```

```
  apiKey: this.apiKey,
  authDomain: this.authDomain,
  projectId: this.projectId,
  storageBucket: this.storageBucket,
  messagingSenderId:
this.messagingSenderId,
  appId: this.appId,
};
```

Next, I declare the constructor in which I insert the `FileService`. Again, I will use the `FileService` to store the details of the uploaded files. Within the constructor, I will initialize the Firebase app. You will need to import `initializeApp` from `'firebase/app'`.

```
constructor(private fileService:
FileService) {
  initializeApp(this.firebaseConfig);
}
```

uploadFiles

Let's create the `uploadFiles` method. It will accept an array of files sent by the frontend application. I will loop through the files and save them one by one to the Firebase storage. For each successful file, I will store its details in the `FileService`.

You can create a method `uploadFile` that only accepts one file instead of an array, but I will leave this as an exercise for you.

```
async uploadFiles(files:
Array<Express.Multer.File>) {
..
}
```

return result

When you upload a file to Firebase, one of the things that is returned is the DownloadUrl of the file. I will create an array called `result` and store all the file details in this array and return it to the frontend after the upload of the files is complete. This way the frontend can read the DownloadUrl of the files and show the end user a preview of the files.
So the first line in the `uploadFiles` method will be:

```
const result = [];
```

The last line in the `uploadFiles` method will be:

```
return result;
```

getStorage

The second step is to get a reference to the storage service:

```
const storage = getStorage();
```

Loop over files

Loop over the files array you received from the frontend application.

```
for (const file of files) {
..
}
```

Unique `fullPath`

Generate a unique `fullPath` for each file with the help of the `uuid` service. You will need to import `extname` from `'path'` and import `{ v4 as uuidv4 }` from `'uuid'`.

```
const fullPath = uuidv4() + '/' +
uuidv4() + extname(file.originalname);
```

`metadata`

When uploading a file, I want to specify the metadata for that file. I want the metadata to include the content type.

```
const metadata = {
  contentType: file.mimetype,
};
```

ref

To upload, download or delete files or retrieve or update metadata, we need to create a reference to the file we want to edit.

We create a reference by calling `ref` from Firebase and passing the `storage` service as the first argument and the `fullPath` as the second argument.

```
const storageRef = ref(storage,
fullPath);
```

uploadBytesResumable

Once we have created the file reference, we can then call the `uploadBytes()` method. I will be using the `uploadBytesResumable()` method.

```
const snapshot = await
uploadBytesResumable(
   storageRef,
   file.buffer,
   metadata,
);
```

Our file has been uploaded successfully.

downloadUrl

Using the `getDownloadURL` method from firebase, we can get the `downloadUrl` of the uploaded file.

```javascript
const downloadUrl = await
getDownloadURL(snapshot.ref);
```

Frontend `fileObj`

I will create a `fileObj` with all the details needed for
the frontend, including the file name, file type, file size,
and downoadUrl. I will push this file into the `result`
array, which I will return to the frontend upon completion.

```javascript
const fileObj = {
  id: undefined,
  originalName: file.originalname,
  mimeType: file.mimetype,
  downloadUrl,
  fullPath,
  size: file.size,
};
```

I will save it first in the database (in our case it is the
`files` array in the `FileService`) so the `id` is
generated then I will add it to the `result` array which
will be returned back to the frontend.

```javascript
const savedFile = await
this.fileService.saveFile(fileObj);
result.push(savedFile);
```

Review

To review, here is the complete definition of the
`uploadFiles` method:

```
async uploadFiles(files:
Array<Express.Multer.File>) {
  const result = [];
  const storage = getStorage();

  for (const file of files) {
    const fullPath = uuidv4() + '/' +
uuidv4() + extname(file.originalname);
    const metadata = {
      contentType: file.mimetype,
    };
    const storageRef = ref(storage,
fullPath);
    const snapshot = await
uploadBytesResumable(
      storageRef,
      file.buffer,
      metadata,
    );
    const downloadUrl = await
getDownloadURL(snapshot.ref);
    const fileObj = {
      originalName: file.originalname,
      mimeType: file.mimetype,
      downloadUrl,
      fullPath,
      size: file.size,
```

```
      };

        const savedFile = await
this.fileService.saveFile(fileObj);
      result.push(savedFile);
    }

    return result;
}
```

deleteFile

I will create another method in the `StorageService` to allow users to delete files. It accepts the fileId as an argument.

```
async deleteFile(id: number) {
  ..
}
```

The first step is to retrieve the saved file object by its id.

```
const file = await
this.fileService.getFile(id);
if (file) {
  ..
} else {
    throw new NotFoundException('File
not found!');
}
```

If found

```
const storage = getStorage();
const fileRef = ref(storage,
file.fullPath);
```

Then delete it from firebase using the fileRef:
```
await deleteObject(fileRef);
```

Next, delete it from the files array in the FileService
```
return await
this.fileService.deleteFile(id);
```
It will delete it and return the deleted file object to the
frontend.

If the file is not found it will throw a not found exception.

Review

Here is the complete definition of the `deleteFile`
method:
```
async deleteFile(id: number) {
  const file = await
this.fileService.getFile(id);
  if (file) {
    const storage = getStorage();
    const fileRef = ref(storage,
file.fullPath);
    await deleteObject(fileRef);
    return await
this.fileService.deleteFile(id);
  } else {
```

```
    throw new NotFoundException('File
not found!');
  }
}
```

Implement StorageController

In the `constructor` inject the `StorageService`:

```
constructor(private storageService:
StorageService) {}
```

uploadFiles endpoint

Create a new endpoint for upload files as follows:

```
@Post('upload-files')
@UseInterceptors(AnyFilesInterceptor())
async uploadFiles(@UploadedFiles()
files: Array<Express.Multer.File>) {
  console.log(files);
  return await
this.storageService.uploadFiles(files);
}
```

- The first line defines the method type `POST` and the path `"upload-files"`.
- The second line is used to intercept files and pass them to the files argument.

- Then I send the files to the `StorageService` to upload them to the Firebase.

`deleteFiles` endpoint

```
@Delete('delete/:id')
async deleteFile(@Param('id') id) {
  return await
this.storageService.deleteFile(id);
}
```

Rooms Module

To see our application in action, I will start from a hotel booking application where the administrator adds rooms. I will create a new room module to see how we can add images for the rooms.

```
nest generate module modules/rooms
```

Rooms Service

```
nest generate service modules/rooms
```

Rooms Controller

```
nest generate controller modules/rooms
```

The rooms controller will have just one method
`addRoom`.

I send the room object in the body of the post request. It
is an object with the properties of type Room and an
additional property roomImages, which is an array of
files to be associated with the room. It is sufficient to
store the file ID, but for performance reasons I also store
the mimeType. This way you can immediately know the
file type image, pdf or whatever without making a
second request for the file type from the files table.

Upload on select

When the user selects files on their device, I
immediately upload them to Firebase and get the
DownloadUrl for them. I then use the DownloadUrl to
preview the files. When the user submits the form, I
send the file IDs as the files are already uploaded to
Firebase and stored in the database.
When the user clicks on the "Delete" button of one of the
images in the preview, I send a separate request to the
backend to delete the file from Firebase and from the
database.

Order

```
<p-orderList
    [value]="roomImages"..
```

The PrimeNG control "OrderList" is bound to the
property roomImages, which is an array of files.
Changing the order of the images in the control by
dragging them, for example, will update the order of the
roomImages array, so you do not need to implement any
extra logic for ordering. Simply binding the OrderList
value to the roomImages array is sufficient.
Just in case you didn't notice, the roomImages contains
the uploaded files after they have been uploaded to
Firebase. The roomImages array is populated when the
result of the POST request is returned. Upon file
selection, I upload the files to Firebase and receive an
array of files that I assign to roomImages.

Append to `roomImages`

Another point to note is that I add to the roomImages
array instead of resetting it with every upload. This way,
you can upload more files, and they will be appended to
the array without clearing the old ones. As you can see,
I use the spread operator to append the new array to the
roomImages array.

```
this.roomImages = [...this.roomImages,
...results];
```

Submit

When the user clicks on the "Save" button, I send the
form values and the roomImages to the backend. The
form values are currently empty, but you can add fields

to it, such as room name, type, number of guests, and so on.

The Frontend

Create a new Angular application. It will have just one page to add a new room. You can add and append room details such as room type and number of beds. I will be using PrimeNG components and icons, so you will need to install the necessary dependencies.

```
npm install primeng primeicons
```

Please check the PrimeNG installation documentation and follow the installation steps.

FileUploadModule

I will use the FileUpload component from primeng. It supports multi file upload and I will use the onSelect event to upload files once they are selected.

OrderListModule

Also from primeng, I will use the OrderList component to display the files in a list with drag and drop ordering. As you have seen, you just bind it to the roomImages array and you are done, no more work is required.

FilesService

I will create a file service to upload and delete files. The
`uploadFiles` method takes the files passed from the
file upload component and sends them to the backend.
It looks as follows:

```
uploadFiles(files: any) {
  const formData = new FormData();
  Array.from(files).forEach((file: any) => {
    formData.append('files[]', file);
  });
  return this.http.post(
    environment.API_URL +
'/storage/upload-files',
    formData
  );
}
```

The `deleteFile` method takes the fileId and deletes
the specified file from both Firebase and the database.
The logic is implemented on the backend; it simply
sends the ID to the backend.

```
deleteFile(id: number) {
  return this.http.delete(environment.API_URL +
'/storage/delete/' + id, {
    headers: {
      'Content-Type': 'application/json',
    },
  });
}
```

How does it work?

The **add-room.component.ts** includes the `onSelectRoomImages` method, which is called when you select files in the file upload component. It sends the files to the backend and adds the results to the roomImages array. The `roomImages` array is bound to the `OrderList` component, so once it receives the new values, they will appear on the screen. When the user submits the form, I send everything to the backend, including the form values and the `roomImages`.
There is also another event handler, `onDeleteRoomImage`, which is attached to the click event of the trash icon for each image. This triggers an explicit call to the backend with the ID of the selected file to be deleted, and it immediately removes the file from the `roomImages` array.

Run the application

Run the backend server
```
nest start
```
Run the frontend server
```
ng serve
```
Go to http://localhost:4200 , it will redirect to http://localhost:4200/add-room automatically.

Congratulations! You have successfully added the upload functionality to your application. You can implement authentication, save to the database, and work confidently with all projects that require file uploads and storage. Good luck!

Conclusion

Congratulations! You have read the book "Angular Observables and Promises: A Practical Guide to Asynchronous Programming". Now you are able to handle all asynchronous scenarios with ease.
Remember that learning Angular is an ongoing process. Practice makes perfect — create your own projects, experiment with the features you have learned, and delve into the extensive online resources.
Thank you for joining me in my exploration of Angular. I wish you the best of luck on your programming journey. Have fun programming and good luck with your applications!

Media Attributions

Memory storage concept illustration
Image by storyset on Freepik

Modern annual report magazine page flyer a company catalog
Image by starline on Freepik

Don't miss out!

Receive an email when Abdelfattah Ragab publishes a new book. It's free and without obligation.

Shippo Integration in Angular: A Step-by-Step Guide to Creating Shipping Functionality

Welcome to the book "Shippo Integration in Angular: A Step-by-Step Guide to Creating Shipping Functionality". In this book, I explain how to integrate Shippo into your Angular application.

Shippo is a multi-carrier shipping solution designed to streamline the shipping process for businesses of all sizes.

By integrating shipping into your application, you can create better types of e-commerce applications.

You will learn how to create the labels, calculate shipping costs, and get the fastest, cheapest, and best rates.

By the end of this book, you will be able to enable shipping in your Angular application and handle all kinds of scenarios.

Let us get started.

Shippo Integration in Angular

A Step-by-Step Guide to Creating
Shipping Functionality

Abdelfattah Ragab

Also by Abdelfattah Ragab

◇ Angular Generative AI

◇ Angular Reactive Forms

◇ Stripe Integration in Angular

◇ CSS Grid Layout

◇ CSS Flexbox Layout

About the Author

Abdelfattah Ragab is a professional software developer with more than 20 years of experience.
https://abdelfattah-ragab.com

About the Publisher

Abdelfattah Ragab is a highly qualified and experienced software developer with over 20 years of experience in the industry. Specializing in front-end development, Abdelfattah Ragab has a deep understanding of Angular, JavaScript, TypeScript, HTML and CSS. Read more at https://abdelfattah-ragab.com